PRO MINDSET®

Be Your Best In Your Biggest Moments

WORKBOOK

CRAIG DOMANN

PRO MINDSET® Workbook

Table of Contents

Chapter 1: The NFL Life

This chapter delves into the realities of life as an NFL player. The media often romanticizes the journey, but behind the scenes, it's filled with challenges, pressures, and constant evaluation. A Pro Mindset helps players navigate this hyper-competitive environment by focusing on their story rather than their circumstances and being their best in the biggest moments.

> " In the NFL's competitive environment, each practice, each rep, is a precious opportunity not to be wasted. "

1. What is the story of your life?

_____

_____

_____

_____

2. Is your story more about you and who you are or about your circumstances and what you do?

_____

_____

_____

_____

3. Do you tend to thrive or struggle in the critical, high-pressure, big moments?

_____

_____

_____

_____

4. Describe a big moment in your life where you excelled or capitalized on the big opportunity. What was the emotion (proud, deserving, relieved, excited, felt seen, etc.) attached to such success?

_____

_____

_____

_____

_____

5. Describe a big opportunity that you failed or were disappointed in your performance. What was the emotion (embarrassed, angry, mad, sad, let someone down, humbled, etc.) attached to such disappointment?

_____

_____

_____

_____

_____

6. Describe a situation where the competition was elite and your competitors were the best of the best. Did you focus more on you or the competition?

_____

_____

_____

_____

_____

7. If you focused on yourself and your game, describe your mindset.

_____

_____

_____

_____

_____

8. If you focused more on the competition, describe how that positively or negatively impacted your own performance.

_____

_____

_____

_____

_____

9. In the NFL, players must make their reps count instead of counting their reps. Describe a situation where you focused more on the fairness, competition, parameters of the opportunity instead of focusing on yourself and your own performance.

_____

_____

_____

_____

_____

Chapter 1: Action Plan

1. Describe or identify a high-pressure situation you are currently facing.

_____

_____

_____

_____

_____

_____

2. List three practical steps you can take to focus more on you and your best performance and not on the circumstances, outcome, or results.

_____

_____

_____

_____

_____

3. Is the goal to perform your best or just do enough to get by (win)?

_____

_____

_____

_____

_____

> " Winning is the normal goal, however, doing your best is always the better goal since you cannot do better than your best. "

Chapter 2: Everyone Has A Story

This chapter delves into the profound impact of the stories we tell ourselves. Our internal narratives are the driving force behind our identity and the trajectory of our future. By consciously rewriting these stories, we can transform our lives, bridging the gap between who we are now and who we aspire to become. Embracing the power of our personal stories allows us to harness our potential and craft a more fulfilling and purposeful life.

> 66 Our story is the power that shapes our reality.
> Changing our story changes our future. 99

1. Current Self-Story: What is the current story you tell yourself about who you are?

_____

_____

_____

_____

2. Reframing Negativity: Identify a negative internal narrative you have. How can you reframe it positively?

_____

_____

_____

_____

3. Impact of External Noise: How has external noise (distractions) influenced your internal story?

_____

_____

_____

_____

4. Overcoming Challenges: Reflect on a time when you successfully overcame a challenge. What story did you tell yourself then?

_____

_____

_____

_____

_____

_____

5. Steps to Rewrite Your Story: What steps can you take to start rewriting your story today?

_____

_____

_____

_____

_____

Chapter 2: Action Plan

1. Identify External Noise: Identify one external noise that has been affecting your story and describe how you will reduce its impact.

_____

_____

_____

_____

_____

_____

2. Empowering Self-Story: Write a new, empowering story about yourself.

_____

_____

_____

_____

_____

_____

3. Goal Setting: Set a goal that aligns with your new story and outline the first steps to achieve it.

_____

_____

_____

_____

_____

_____

> " Understanding and reshaping the stories we tell ourselves is a powerful tool for personal growth. By consciously crafting narratives that reflect our strengths and potential, we can steer our lives in a direction that aligns with our true aspirations and values. "

Chapter 3: Stand in Your Worth

This chapter focuses on the importance of recognizing and standing in your worth. Facing adversity and staying true to your identity are crucial to maintaining self-belief and resilience.

>  Standing in and owning your worth
> is simply you being you.
> You be you.

1. Describe a situation where you felt your worth was challenged. How did you respond?

_____

_____

_____

_____

_____

2. How do desperation, comparison, dishonesty, and perfection impact your sense of worth?

_____

_____

_____

_____

_____

3. Reflect on a time when you stood firm in your worth despite external pressures. What was the outcome?

_____

_____

_____

_____

4. How can you remind yourself of your worth daily?

_____

_____

_____

_____

_____

5. What strategies can you implement to overcome identity killers such as desperation or comparison?

_____

_____

_____

_____

_____

Chapter 3: Action Plan

1. Identify a current challenge to your worth and describe how you will stand firm in your identity.

_____

_____

_____

_____

_____

_____

2. List three affirmations that reinforce your worth.

_____

_____

_____

_____

_____

_____

3. Outline a plan to reduce the impact of one identity killer in your life.

_____

_____

_____

_____

_____

_____

 Standing in your worth means embracing your true self and affirming your value, regardless of external pressures. By implementing these strategies and regularly reflecting on your worth, you can build a strong foundation of self-belief and resilience.

Chapter 4: Visualization – Making Yourself the Star of Your Own Movie

Visualization is a mental rehearsal technique that helps you achieve your goals by creating vivid and detailed images of your success. By imagining yourself as the protagonist in your personal movie, you align your mindset and actions with your desired outcomes. This chapter will guide you through the process of visualizing your success, turning your goals into a cinematic experience where you are the hero of your own story.

> **66** The mind is everything.
> What you think you become. **99**

1. What specific goal or vision do you want to achieve? Define your goal in clear, precise terms. What does success look like for you?

_____

_____

_____

_____

2. What key scenes will your personal movie include? Identify the significant milestones and challenges in your journey. How do these events shape your path to success?

_____

_____

_____

_____

_____

3. How do you envision yourself handling obstacles and achieving success? Picture your actions and responses to challenges. What strengths and qualities will you exhibit?

_____

_____

_____

_____

4. What details will make your visualization more vivid and realistic? Consider the environment, sensory experiences, and emotions. How can you enhance the realism of your mental imagery?

_____

_____

_____

_____

5. How often will you practice visualization, and what tools will you use? Decide on a regular schedule for your visualization practice. Will you use vision boards, recordings, or other aids?

_____

_____

_____

_____

Chapter 4: Action Plan

1. Define Your Goal
- Write down your specific goal or vision.
- Ensure it is clear, measurable, and achievable.

_____

_____

_____

_____

_____

_____

2. Create a Script
- Outline the major scenes of your personal movie.
- Describe each scene in detail, including challenges and victories.

_____

_____

_____

_____

_____

3. Schedule Visualization Sessions
- Dedicate 10-15 minutes daily to visualization.
- Choose a quiet space where you can focus without interruptions.

_____

_____

_____

_____

4. Engage All Senses
- Incorporate visual, auditory, and emotional elements into your visualization.
- Imagine the sights, sounds, and feelings associated with achieving your goal.

_____

_____

_____

_____

5. Use Visualization Tools
- Consider using vision boards, motivational imagery, or audio recordings to enhance your visualization practice.

_____

_____

_____

_____

6. Monitor Your Progress

- Keep a journal to track your thoughts and feelings during your visualization sessions.
- Note any changes in your behavior or mindset as you progress.

_____

_____

_____

_____

7. Adjust and Refine

- Periodically review and adjust your script based on your evolving goals and experiences.
- Stay flexible and open to modifying your visualization as needed.

_____

_____

_____

_____

 By turning your goals into a vivid, cinematic experience where you play the leading role, visualization becomes a dynamic tool that propels you toward success. Embrace this practice, and let your personal movie inspire and guide you on your journey to achieving your dreams.

Chapter 5: Raise Your Standard

Raising your standards is about setting higher expectations for yourself and your performance and committing to meeting these expectations consistently. It requires a dedication to self-improvement and an unwavering commitment to refusing mediocrity. By continually striving for excellence, you can transform your life and achieve greater success and fulfillment.

> "Raising your standards means refusing to accept mediocrity and continuously striving for excellence."

1. Identify Areas for Improvement: What areas of your life do you believe you need a higher standard?

_____

_____

_____

_____

_____

2. Reflect on Past Success: Describe a time when raising your standards led to significant improvement.

_____

_____

_____

_____

3. Accountability: How can you hold yourself accountable to higher standards?

_____

_____

_____

_____

_____

4. Support Systems and Habits: What support systems or habits can help you maintain these elevated standards?

_____

_____

_____

_____

_____

5. Settling: Identify any areas where you've been settling for less than your best. How can you change this?

_____

_____

_____

_____

_____

_____

Chapter 5: Action Plan

1. Set a New Standard: Choose one area of your life where you want to raise your standard and outline specific steps to achieve it.

_____

_____

_____

_____

_____

2. Monitor and Evaluate Progress: Create a plan to regularly monitor and evaluate your progress.

_____

_____

_____

_____

_____

3. Immediate Actions: List three actions you will take this week to raise your standards.

_____

_____

_____

_____

_____

_____

> **"** By setting and maintaining higher standards, you create a pathway to achieving excellence in every aspect of your life. Regularly evaluating your progress and making necessary adjustments ensures that you stay on track and continue to strive for your best. **"**

Chapter 6: Plug Into Your Purpose

The cornerstone of discipline and willpower lies in having a clear vision for your future. Yet, you cannot formulate this vision until you first connect with your purpose. Your purpose is your "why," your calling, and that person or cause you would defend at all costs.

> **“** No purpose means no vision. No vision means no self-discipline. You must tap into your purpose to cast a vision for your future and support it with self-discipline. **”**

1. What do you believe is your life's purpose?

_____

_____

_____

_____

_____

_____

2. What activities or causes ignite your passion and make you feel most alive?

_____

_____

_____

_____

_____

3. Who or what would you be willing to fight for, even against great odds?

_____

_____

_____

_____

_____

4. How does your current career or life path align with your purpose?

_____

_____

_____

_____

_____

5. Describe a moment when you felt deeply connected to your purpose. What were you doing?

_____

_____

_____

_____

_____

6. Identify an obstacle that has kept you from fully embracing your purpose. How can you overcome it?

_____

_____

_____

_____

_____

7. What small steps can you take today to start living more in line with your purpose?

_____

_____

_____

_____

_____

Chapter 6: Action Plan

1. Define Your Purpose: Write a clear and concise statement of your purpose.

_____

_____

_____

_____

_____

2. Align Your Actions: Identify one daily activity that does not align with your purpose and plan to replace it with one that does.

_____

_____

_____

_____

_____

3. Vision Board: Create a vision board that visually represents your purpose and the future you desire.

_____

_____

_____

_____

Chapter 6: Action Plan

4. Accountability Partner: Find someone who shares or supports your vision and establish a regular check-in routine to stay on track.

_____

_____

_____

_____

_____

5. Reflect and Adjust: Set aside time each week to reflect on your actions and ensure they align with your purpose. Make adjustments as needed.

_____

_____

_____

_____

_____

> 66 By grounding yourself in your purpose, you can cultivate the discipline and willpower needed to create a vision for your future and take actionable steps toward achieving it. 99

Chapter 7: Show Up

Showing up means being fully present and committed in every moment. It's about consistently giving your best effort, regardless of the circumstances. When you show up with full presence and engagement, you open the door to personal growth, stronger relationships, and greater achievements.

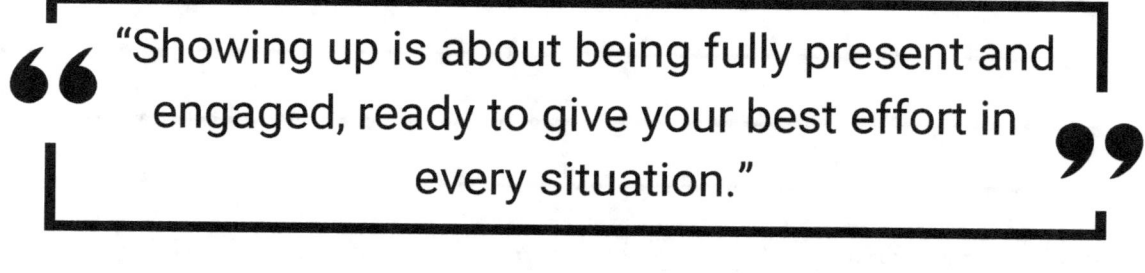

"Showing up is about being fully present and engaged, ready to give your best effort in every situation."

1. Personal Meaning: What does it mean to you to "show up" in your life?

_____

_____

_____

_____

2. Reflect on Success: Reflect on a time when you showed up fully. What was the outcome?

_____

_____

_____

_____

_____

3. Consistency in Challenges: How can you ensure that you show up consistently, even in challenging times?

_____

_____

_____

_____

_____

4. Identify Areas for Improvement: What are some areas of your life where you feel you need to show up more?

_____

_____

_____

_____

_____

5. Supportive Habits: What habits or routines can you develop to support your commitment to showing up?

_____

_____

_____

_____

_____

Chapter 7: Action Plan

1. Choose an Area to Improve: Identify one area of your life where you want to show up more fully and describe how you will do it.

_____

_____

_____

_____

_____

_____

2. Develop Daily Habits: List three daily habits that will help you be more present and engaged.

_____

_____

_____

_____

_____

_____

3. Plan for Regular Review: Outline a plan to review and adjust your commitment regularly.

_____

_____

_____

_____

_____

_____

> By fully committing to showing up in all aspects of your life, you create opportunities for growth and success. Establishing daily habits and routines that support this commitment ensures you remain engaged and present, even when faced with challenges. Regularly reviewing your progress and making adjustments will keep you on track to consistently show up and give your best effort.

Chapter 8: Performance Bubble

The concept of the performance bubble involves creating an optimal environment where you can perform at your best by blocking out distractions and focusing intensely on your goals. By cultivating this bubble, you can enhance your productivity, creativity, and overall effectiveness. Additionally, embracing a performance bubble fosters belief in yourself, confidence in your abilities, and a sense of peace and freedom that further propels your success.

> " Creating a performance bubble allows you to focus intensely on your goals, free from distractions. "

1. Identify Distractions: What distractions currently prevent you from performing at your best?

_____

_____

_____

_____

_____

2. Creating Your Bubble: How can you create a "performance bubble" in your daily life?

_____

_____

_____

_____

3. Reflect on Focus: Reflect on a time when you were able to focus intensely on a task. What strategies helped you?

_____

_____

_____

_____

_____

4. Environmental Changes: What changes can you make to your environment to reduce distractions?

_____

_____

_____

_____

_____

5. Consistency: How can you maintain this performance bubble consistently?

_____

_____

_____

_____

_____

Chapter 8: Action Plan

1. Specific Goal and Bubble Creation: Identify a specific goal and outline how you will create a performance bubble to achieve it.

_____

_____

_____

_____

_____

_____

2. Minimize Distractions: List three steps to minimize distractions in your environment.

_____

_____

_____

_____

_____

_____

3. Daily Routine: Develop a routine to enter your performance bubble daily.

_____

_____

_____

_____

_____

_____

> By establishing a performance bubble, you set the stage for achieving peak performance. Identifying distractions and taking proactive steps to minimize them will help you maintain focus and stay committed to your goals. Developing and sticking to a daily routine ensures you can consistently access this heightened state of productivity. In turn, this focused approach bolsters your belief in yourself, builds confidence in your abilities, and fosters a sense of peace and freedom essential for sustained success.

Chapter 9: Be In The Moment

Being present means fully engaging in the current moment without distraction. This practice not only enhances your focus but also reduces stress and improves overall performance. By committing to being present, you cultivate a more mindful and productive life.

> **Being present is about fully engaging in the current moment, enhancing your focus and reducing stress.**

1. Current Practice: How do you currently practice being present in your daily life?

_____

_____

_____

_____

_____

2. Impact of Presence: Reflect on a time when you were fully present. What impact did it have?

_____

_____

_____

_____

3. Challenges: What are the biggest challenges you face in being present?

_____

_____

_____

_____

_____

4. Mindfulness Practices: How can you incorporate mindfulness practices into your routine?

_____

_____

_____

_____

_____

5. Expected Benefits: What benefits do you expect to gain from being more present?

_____

_____

_____

_____

_____

Chapter 9: Action Plan

1. Mindfulness Practice: Identify one mindfulness practice you will start this week to improve your presence.

_____

_____

_____

_____

_____

_____

2. Daily Triggers: List three triggers that remind you to be present throughout the day.

_____

_____

_____

_____

_____

_____

3. Review Progress: Outline a plan to review your progress in being present regularly.

_____

_____

_____

_____

_____

_____

> " By embracing the practice of being present, you can significantly enhance your daily experiences. Identifying mindfulness practices and incorporating them into your routine will help you stay focused and reduce stress. Regularly reviewing your progress ensures you remain committed to cultivating a more mindful and fulfilling life. "

Chapter 10: Pro Mindset: ReThink Your Reality

The final chapter focuses on transforming your thoughts into reality through the consistent application of Pro Mindset principles. It's about making your goals achievable by combining disciplined action with a mindset geared towards excellence. By rethinking your reality, you can align your actions with your aspirations and achieve extraordinary results.

> **"** Transforming your thoughts into reality requires disciplined action and consistent application of Pro Mindset principles. **"**

1. Significant Goal: What is a significant goal you have been working towards?

_____

_____

_____

_____

2. Influence of Thoughts: How have your thoughts influenced your progress toward this goal?

_____

_____

_____

_____

3. Actions Taken: What specific actions have you taken to move your thoughts into reality?

_____

_____

_____

_____

_____

4. Overcoming Setbacks: Reflect on any setbacks you've encountered. How did you overcome them, and what did you learn?

_____

_____

_____

_____

_____

5. Consistent Application: How can you ensure that you continue to apply Pro Mindset principles to achieve your goals?

_____

_____

_____

_____

_____

Chapter 10: Action Plan

1. Goal Identification: Identify a goal you want to achieve and outline the steps to transform this goal from thought to reality.

_____

_____

_____

_____

_____

_____

2. Weekly Actions: List three actions you will take this week to advance towards this goal.

_____

_____

_____

_____

_____

_____

3. Review Process: Develop a review process to track your progress and adjust your actions as needed.

_____

_____

_____

_____

_____

_____

> By embracing the Pro Mindset and consistently applying its principles, you can transform your thoughts into reality. Identifying your goals, taking deliberate actions, and continuously reviewing your progress will ensure you stay on track. This disciplined approach not only helps in achieving your goals but also in maintaining a mindset that constantly strives for excellence.